VOYAGES
IN ENGLISH
Writing and Grammar

Grade 5 Practice Book

Elaine de Chantal Brookes

Patricia Healey

Irene Kervick

Catherine Irene Masino

Anne B. McGuire

Adrienne Saybolt

LOYOLAPRESS.

ISBN-10: 0-8294-2106-8
ISBN-13: 978-0-8294-2106-4

LOYOLAPRESS.

3441 N. Ashland Avenue
Chicago, Illinois 60657
(800) 621-1008
www.loyolapress.com

Bang / Brainerd, MN USA / 05-10 / 5th printing

CONTENTS

CHAPTER 5

Writing: Book Reports
Grammar: Adverbs, Prepositions, Conjunctions, Interjections

CHAPTER 6

Writing: Creative Writing (Tall Tales)
Grammar: Sentences

CHAPTER 7

Writing: Persuasive Writing
Grammar: Punctuation, Capitalization

CHAPTER 8

Writing: Research Reports
Grammar: Diagramming

CHAPTER

1

Sentence Variety

● **Change these sentences to make them more interesting. You can change the order of the words, add words, or change the sentences into exclamations or questions.**

1. I looked up and saw a star shoot across the sky.

   _____

2. I've always wanted to go camping in Yosemite.

   _____

3. Terrance jumped after he heard the crash.

   _____

4. It's dangerous to swim if there's no lifeguard on duty.

   _____

5. We tiptoed past the baby's room.

   _____

● **Rewrite this paragraph to make it more interesting. Use a variety of sentences.**

> I heard the ball connect with the bat—crack! I dropped the bat and ran! I had hit a grand slam! The crowd cheered as I circled the bases! My heart was pounding! I was floating on air! I don't know how I stayed on my feet! The other players ran toward me! I knew we had won the game!

_____

_____

_____

_____

_____

Nouns as Objects

● **Circle the letter under the heading that describes the italicized noun in each sentence.**

	Direct Object	Object of a Preposition
1. Our baseball team won the *championship*.	T	M
2. James brought a pie to the *picnic*.	O	H
3. Mr. Shaw gave his speech in the *morning*.	T	E
4. Stacy wrote a story about summer *vacation*.	A	L
5. Tia rode her *bike* to school.	E	R
6. Flowers in the *garden* are blooming.	H	T
7. My teacher gave the class a surprise *quiz*.	T	S
8. Max dug up the *bone* in the backyard.	E	O
9. Tyrone mailed his pen pal a *postcard*.	R	P
10. I did the weekend chores for my *mother*.	D	E

● **Now write the circled letters, in order, on the numbered lines below. If your answers are correct, you will reveal the answer to the riddle.**

What appears twice in a week and once in a year but never in a day?

Answer: ___ ___ ___
        1   2   3

___ ___ ___ ___ ___ ___ ___
4   5   6   7   8   9   10

CHAPTER
1

Exact Words

● **Replace the words in italics with more exact words.**

1. "Shh! The baby is sleeping," Mom *said*.   _____

2. The *big* bear wandered into our camp.   _____

3. The queen lives in a magnificent *place*.   _____

4. The wind made the crisp, orange leaves *move*
   on the branches.   _____

5. Boo's black fur was long and *soft*.   _____

● **Rewrite this paragraph, changing the italicized words to more exact words.**

> *We* watched as the race cars sped quickly around the racetrack.
> *Their* engines sounded as they went by. *They* were so loud that
> I could barely hear myself *yelling*. The crowd cheered excitedly
> as Car 55 moved ahead of the pack. *It* shone brightly in the sun
> like a flash of lightning. *We* yelled as it crossed the finish line.
> The black-and-white checkered flag flapping signaled the end
> of the race.

_____

_____

_____

_____

_____

_____

_____

_____

Name Olivia Wynkoop   **Date** _____

CHAPTER 1

Words Used as Nouns or as Adjectives

● Use each word in the box to complete two of the sentences below. For each sentence write *noun* or *adjective* to show how the word is used.

> football   ocean   mountain   lemon   magazine

1. Huge, frothy _ocean_ waves crashed on the sandy shore.   noun

2. This sports _magazine_ contains several good articles about basketball.   noun

3. The high school _football_ game went into overtime.   adj

4. The Sierras, a _mountain_ range in California, have redwood trees.   adj

5. The view from the peak of the _mountain_ was beautiful.   noun

6. He caught the _football_ and ran down the field.   noun

7. My favorite dessert is _lemon_ meringue pie.   adj

8. I read a _magazine_ article about how to start a coin collection.   adj

9. She gazed at the endless stretch of blue _ocean_ before her.   noun

10. You may cut up that _lemon_ for the iced tea.   noun

● For each word write two sentences. In the first sentence use the word as a noun. In the second sentence use the same word as an adjective.

11. sports

_____

_____

12. gold

_____

_____

Name _____ Date _____

Self-Assessment

● Check *Always, Sometimes,* or *Never* to respond to each statement.

Writing	Always	Sometimes	Never
I can identify the features of a personal narrative.			
I can write an introduction, a body, and a conclusion for a personal narrative and present events in time order.			
I can use a variety of sentences in my writing.			
I can use a dictionary thesaurus and an indexed thesaurus to find words.			
I can use exact words to make my writing more interesting.			

Grammar	Always	Sometimes	Never
I can identify and use common nouns and proper nouns.			
I can identify and form singular nouns and plural nouns.			
I can identify and form possessive nouns.			
I can identify and use collective, count, and noncount nouns.			
I can identify and use nouns as subjects and subject complements.			
I can identify and use nouns as objects.			
I can identify and use nouns as indirect objects.			
I can identify and use nouns in direct address.			
I can identify and use words used as nouns and as verbs.			
I can identify and use words used as nouns and as adjectives.			

● **Write the most helpful thing you learned in this chapter.**

_____

_____

_____

CHAPTER 2

Singular Pronouns and Plural Pronouns

● **Replace each word or words in italics with a personal pronoun from the word box. Rewrite the sentence using the pronoun. Then write S for singular or P for plural above the pronoun to identify it.**

we	us	they	them	he	she
her	I	him	you	me	it

1. *Maria* is giving a speech on birds of the rain forest.

   _____

2. *Kaitlyn and I* wrote a report about the big cats of Africa.

   _____

3. Mr. Ramos gave *Jarvis* extra credit for tutoring.

   _____

4. Jess asked *Melanie and me* about the bake sale.

   _____

5. Did you tell *Melanie* about the book with magic cats?

   _____

6. *These stories* are the best I've read so far this year.

   _____

● **Use personal pronouns from the word box to write four sentences about you and your friends. Use at least one pronoun in each sentence. Identify it as singular or plural.**

7. _____

8. _____

9. _____

10. _____

CHAPTER 2

Personal Pronouns

● **Circle the pronoun in each sentence. Write *singular* or *plural* to identify its number. Then write *first, second,* or *third* to identify its person.**

	Singular/Plural	Person
1. Chelsea gave me flowers for my birthday.	_____	_____
2. She said the flowers came from Mom's garden.	_____	_____
3. Theo pointed to where we could leave the coats.	_____	_____
4. They were in a big pile on the bed.	_____	_____
5. Manuel decided to give him the gold medal.	_____	_____
6. Bianca and I both scored on the home run.	_____	_____
7. Did you see Bianca slide into home plate, Linda?	_____	_____
8. We heard the crowd cheering our names.	_____	_____
9. The coaches named her Most Valuable Player.	_____	_____
10. Did Bianca show them the trophy?	_____	_____
11. The coaches may want to display it in a trophy case.	_____	_____
12. Bianca's family was happy that they came to see the game.	_____	_____

What Makes a Good How-to Article?

CHAPTER 2

● **Read the how-to article. Then answer the questions.**

> Did you know that you can train your cat to shake your hand? Most people train their dogs but often don't consider training their cats. Cats are very smart and learn quickly. First make sure you have lots of tasty treats as rewards. Then place a treat in your hand. Next hold your hand in front of your cat until it reaches up for the treat. Reward your cat with the treat. If you repeat this activity many times, soon your cat will reach up to "shake" your hand even without a treat. You will have trained your cat to associate a reward with "shaking" your hand. You can train your cat to perform many other tricks, too. All it takes is a few treats and some patience!

1. What is the topic of this paragraph?
   a. choosing a pet
   b. training your cat
   c. grooming your cat

2. Who is the audience for this paragraph?
   a. pet groomers
   b. children
   c. cat lovers

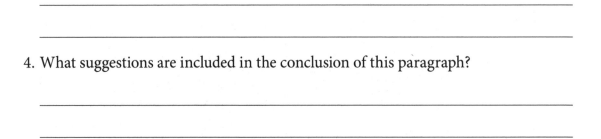

3. Read the introductory sentence to this paragraph. Did it grab your attention? Why?

   _____

   _____

4. What suggestions are included in the conclusion of this paragraph?

   _____

   _____

CHAPTER
2

Order, Accuracy, and Completeness

● **Read each set of directions. Are they in logical order? If not, reorder them by writing the correct numbers on the lines.**

1. Put pasta in the boiling water.   _____

2. Put the pot of water on the stove.   _____

3. Put water in the pot.   _____

4. Pour cooked pasta into a strainer.   _____

5. Let water come to a boil.   _____

6. Let pasta cook for five minutes.   _____

What is the topic of these directions? _____

1. Save your changes.   _____

2. Place the cursor where you want to paste the text.   _____

3. Find the text you want to select.   _____

4. Cut the highlighted text.   _____

5. Paste the selected text.   _____

6. Highlight the text.   _____

What is the topic of these directions? _____

● **Choose an activity for which you can write simple directions. Copy a blank sequence chart from page 137 onto a separate sheet of paper. Write the activity name in the *Topic* section. Write the directions on the chart. In the *Conclusion* section, write a brief conclusion that might appear in a how-to article.**

CHAPTER

2 Indirect Objects

● **Replace the italicized noun or phrase in each sentence with a pronoun used as an indirect object. Rewrite the sentence with the pronoun.**

1. Greece gave *the people of the world* the Olympic Games.

   _____

2. Men and boys showed *the Greek citizens* their talents in sports.

   _____

3. We paid *Kate* twenty dollars for mowing the lawn.

   _____

4. I promised *Mr. Tien* an extra-credit assignment this week.

   _____

5. Did you read *baby Jenna* a story before bedtime?

   _____

6. Ms. Santos gave *Lisa and I* a good grade for our presentation.

   _____

7. The principal presented *our team* the spelling trophy.

   _____

8. Maya sent *Jake* many postcards during her travels in Europe.

   _____

9. I bought *my sister* a gift for her birthday.

   _____

10. Manuel offered *the stray cat* a big bowl of food and fresh water.

   _____

CHAPTER
2

Uses of Pronouns

● **Circle the pronoun that correctly completes each sentence.**

1. Chan and (me   I) are trying out for the tennis team this year.

2. Will you lend (me   I) your tennis racquet?

3. That copy of *Tennis Tips* belongs to (they   them).

4. I told (she   her) about my plan.

5. My tennis instructor is (her   she).

6. (Them   They) are good tennis players.

7. Some people saw (I   me) on the tennis court.

8. Tell (them   they) about the tennis team tryouts.

9. Does this towel belong to (him   he)?

10. (Him   He) played a brilliant game.

11. We cheered for (him   he) until our throats were hoarse.

12. The students already on the tennis team are (they   them).

CHAPTER 2

Transition Words

● Circle six transition words and phrases in this paragraph. Hint: The first transition word is *First*.

> Have you ever made your own foaming volcano? It's easy to do and lots of fun! First gather the necessary items: baking soda, vinegar, a paper cup, clay, and a tablespoon. Then build a clay volcano around the paper cup. The cup will hold your "lava." After that place a couple of tablespoons of baking soda in the cup. Next pour in some vinegar. Now watch what happens! Afterward, write your observations in your science journal.

● Rewrite these directions in paragraph form. Add transition words and phrases to make the directions clear.

Yummy French Toast

1. Gather some bread, eggs, milk, butter, cinnamon, and vanilla.
2. Beat together 2 eggs, 1/3 cup milk, and 1/2 teaspoon vanilla.
3. Place a pat of butter in the pan to melt.
4. Dip bread in egg mixture and place in hot, buttered pan.
5. Fry bread on each side until golden brown.
6. Sprinkle frying bread with cinnamon.

_____

_____

_____

_____

_____

_____

_____

_____

_____

CHAPTER
2

Possessives

- **Circle the possessive pronoun in each sentence. Then write *singular* or *plural* to identify it.**

1. Rafael, these markers are yours.   _____

2. The task of coaching students was his.   _____

3. Hers is the skirt with little yellow flowers.   _____

4. Ours are the chocolate chip cookies.   _____

5. This new car is theirs.   _____

6. This drawing is mine.   _____

- **Replace each italicized word or group of words with a possessive pronoun. Write the pronoun on the line.**

7. Maria, what was *your story* about?   _____

8. *Bob and Pat's story* was about astronauts.   _____

9. *Tamika's cat* likes to chase squirrels.   _____

10. *Deshaun's and my desks* are near the front
    of the classroom.   _____

11. *My house* is the one on the corner.   _____

12. This model of the solar system is *Jason's*.   _____

CHAPTER 2

Intensive Pronouns, Reflexive Pronouns

● **Underline the intensive or reflexive pronoun in each sentence.**

1. The students themselves raised money for kids in the hospital.

2. We gave ourselves two weekends to plan for the bake sale.

3. I myself baked some oatmeal cookies.

4. The principal herself made some cookies.

5. Do you make these tasty-looking muffins yourself?

● **Complete each sentence with an intensive or a reflexive pronoun. Make it agree with the italicized noun.**

6. *We* set _____ a goal of five hundred dollars.

7. *Jake* _____ sold over 50 dollars of baked goods.

8. *I* _____ designed the posters for the sale.

9. *The students* organized the sale _____ .

10. *Keisha* made four-dozen cupcakes _____ .

11. *We* surprised _____ by raising over seven hundred dollars to give to the children.

12. The cookie *raffle* _____ raised over one hundred dollars.

CHAPTER 2

Synonyms

● **For each word write a more interesting synonym from the word box.**
 Use a dictionary if you need help.

ecstatic	generous	surly	mournful	terrified
arrogant	ascend	chortle	adore	discover

1. find _____

2. rise _____

3. excited _____

4. sad _____

5. scared _____

6. love _____

7. proud _____

8. giving _____

9. grouchy _____

10. laugh _____

● **Circle the word in each row that is not a synonym of the other words.**

11.	small	tiny	little	shallow
12.	proper	third	right	correct
13.	above	beneath	under	below
14.	fragile	delicate	breakable	sturdy
15.	method	way	chatter	manner
16.	attempt	stop	halt	end

© Loyola Press

CHAPTER 2

Antecedents

● **Circle the pronouns in each paragraph. Then underline the antecedent the pronoun refers to. Draw an arrow from each pronoun to its antecedent.**

The early leaders of the United States wanted to choose a national bird. They wanted it to be a noble and fearless bird. Ben Franklin suggested the turkey. He said the turkey was brave. But his colleagues wanted the bald eagle. They claimed it was native to North America and a strong symbol of freedom. So the bald eagle was chosen. It shows up on many American items, such as coins.

Another symbol of freedom is the Statue of Liberty. It was a gift from the French. They wanted to show their friendship to the United States. The French sculptor Frederic Bartholdi was hired to design the statue. He was supposed to be finished in 1876, but a lack of money put the project in doubt. Lotteries, auctions, and even prizefights helped to raise money for it. When the statue was finally brought to America, it was in 350 pieces! Today Liberty stands 152 feet tall. She has an index finger eight feet long!

CHAPTER 2 Pronouns and Contractions

● **Rewrite each sentence. Write the contraction for each italicized group of words.**

1. Mario learned that *he is* getting an A on his science project.

   _____

2. *They are* waiting for us in the lobby of the hotel.

   _____

3. Did you know *you have* been resting for two hours?

   _____

4. "*We are* ready to go," Kendra said with a smile.

   _____

5. *I will* help you pack the car for your trip.

   _____

6. Josh and Lashauna said *they will* be here in one hour.

   _____

7. My sister said *she is* getting a soccer scholarship.

   _____

8. *We will* go and see her play as often as we can.

   _____

9. *It is* a story about two friends who go on an incredible adventure.

   _____

10. *I have* been studying for my math test all weekend.

   _____

CHAPTER 2

Using the Internet

● Read each topic. Then write the three-letter Internet extension from the box that tells what kind of address you would most likely look for to research the topic.

> .mil   .org   .com   .gov   .edu

1. schedule of classes for a community college   _____

2. where to donate used clothes   _____

3. the Navy's achievements during WWII   _____

● Read the Web site information. Then answer the questions.

http://www.tigersinc.org

Tigers, Inc.

Tigers, Inc., is a non-profit organization that believes in the care and preservation of tigers in the wild. This organization was founded in 1983 to find ways of saving endangered tigers. Tigers are close to extinction in many parts of the world. We are devoted to keeping this proud and beautiful animal safe from hunters. Our Web site, created in 2001, has helped us obtain thousands of donations. Click on the links below to find out more about tigers and their preservation. Thank you!

—Ms. Mia Harris, Program Director and Zoologist

> Kinds of Tigers   Habitats   Food   Babies
> Hunting   Preservation   How You Can Help   Contact us

4. What is the purpose of this Web site: to sell, to entertain, or to inform?

_____

5. Do you think this site will include facts that you can check in other sources? Why?

_____

_____

CHAPTER 2

Demonstrative Pronouns, Interrogative Pronouns

● **Write a demonstrative pronoun to complete each sentence. Follow the directions in parentheses.**

1. _____ are good references for the report. (near, plural)

2. Is _____ a scary ride? (far, singular)

3. _____ are the students I was telling you about. (far, plural)

4. _____ are delicious! (near, plural)

5. _____ is the kitten I want to adopt. (near, singular)

6. Will _____ take me to Oak Avenue? (far, singular)

● **Circle the interrogative pronoun that correctly completes each sentence.**

7. (Whom   Who) saw the shooting stars last night?

8. (What   Whose) have you seen through your telescope?

9. (Whom   Who) does Mia prefer?

10. (Whose   What) was the great report on volcanoes?

11. (Who   Whom) will Ms. Sutton choose?

12. (What   Who) happened after the game?

13. (Who   Whose) is the backpack with the red stripe?

Self-Assessment

● Check *Always, Sometimes,* or *Never* to respond to each statement.

Writing	Always	Sometimes	Never
I can identify the features of a how-to article.			
I can write the steps of a how-to article in logical order and make them complete and accurate.			
I can identify and use transition words.			
I can identify and use synonyms.			
I can identify and use reliable information on the Internet.			

Grammar	Always	Sometimes	Never
I can identify and use singular pronouns and plural pronouns.			
I can identify and use personal pronouns.			
I can identify and use subject pronouns.			
I can identify and use object pronouns.			
I can identify and use pronouns used as indirect objects.			
I can identify and use pronouns correctly.			
I can identify and use possessives.			
I can identify and use intensive pronouns and reflexive pronouns.			
I can show agreement between pronouns and their antecedents.			
I can identify and use pronouns as part of contractions.			
I can identify and use demonstrative pronouns and interrogative pronouns.			

● Write the most helpful thing you learned in this chapter.

_____

_____

_____

CHAPTER 3

What Makes a Good Business Letter?

● **Read the business letter. Then follow the directions.**

555 Lily Lane
Big Mountain, UT 44190

June 10, 20‍7‍0

Mr. Justin Bright
Director of Special Programs
The Children's Natural History Museum
1172 Daley Drive
Big Mountain, UT 44190

Dear Mr. Bright:

I am a counselor at the Wyatt Park Summer Camp. I am interested in bringing a group of children to your museum. I think a visit to the natural history museum would be educational and would also inspire some great discussions and fun projects back at camp.

I was hoping that you could arrange a special tour for about 45 children sometime in the month of August. In addition to the tour, I would like to have the children participate in one of your special "dinosaur dig" activities. I've heard they're super cool!

Let me know a good day for the gang to swing by. I am looking forward to it, and I know the children will too.

Thank you so much for your time and consideration.

Sincerely yours,

Miranda Reeves

Miranda Reeves
Head Counselor
Wyatt Park Summer Camp

1. Label each part of this business letter. Write your labels in the boxes.

2. Underline the two sentences in this letter that seem too informal.

3. Rewrite the two sentences that are too informal using a more formal tone.

_____

_____

© Loyola Press

CHAPTER
3

Articles

● Write the correct indefinite article, *a* or *an*, before each item.

1. _____ orange

2. _____ eagle

3. _____ jacket

4. _____ angel

5. _____ telephone

6. _____ student

7. _____ umbrella

8. _____ beach

9. _____ hamburger

10. _____ igloo

● Underline the articles in each sentence. Then write *D* for definite or *I* for indefinite above each article to identify it.

11. The palm trees waved slowly in the cool breeze.

12. I found a lost puppy behind the trashcans.

13. The money is inside an orange envelope.

14. An apple is a good snack.

15. Justin threw a football 40 yards down the field.

16. That was the best movie I've seen in over a year.

CHAPTER 3
Repetition of Articles

● **Add appropriate articles where they are needed in each sentence. You do not need to write an article on every line.**

1. _____ friend and _____ teammate, Louis, helped me walk off the field.

2. _____ writer and _____ poet gave separate presentations after school.

3. _____ dancer, _____ organist, and _____ singer are all in the show.

4. _____ sculptor and _____ teacher showed us the exhibit himself.

5. She worked as both _____ writer and _____ illustrator of this book.

6. _____ pet groomer and _____ trainer both worked wonders for my dog.

7. _____ advisor and _____ coach named Staci gave us a tour of the gym.

8. Brandon used _____ wrench and _____ hammer to fix the window.

9. As _____ athlete, _____ scholar, and _____ volunteer, Alejandra does it all.

10. I saw _____ eagle, _____ bear, and _____ ape at the zoo.

● **Write a sentence using two or more nouns joined by *and*. Refer to two or more people, places, or things.**

_____

_____

● **Write a sentence using two or more nouns joined by *and*. Refer to one person, place, or thing.**

_____

_____

CHAPTER 3
Purpose

● **Use a word from the word box to complete each sentence. You will not use all of the words.**

beginning	action	complaint	information
respond	informally	request	heading
middle	clearly	ending	salutation

1. Remember to state the purpose of your business letter quickly and

   _____.

2. Specify what _____ you want the company, organization, or person to take.

3. State the purpose of your letter in the _____ of the letter.

4. The middle of a business letter includes _____ that explains more about the letter's purpose.

5. End a business letter by asking the receiver to act on or _____ to your request.

● **Read the sections from business letters. Identify the purpose of each letter by writing *Order a product, Inquire or request,* or *Complain*.**

6. I was very disappointed by the lack of help I received from the staff of Blue Sky Airlines. _____

7. Please send 25 copies of the textbook *Legends of American History*, 6th edition, to the following address: Tyler Elementary School, 3005 Stilton Lane, Tyler, IL 99235. _____

8. Because of your many travels through South America and your experiences with these cultures, we would be honored to have you speak at our annual luncheon. _____

9. Four of the six glasses shipped to me were broken. This is the second time I have received damaged merchandise from your company. _____

CHAPTER 3

Demonstrative Adjectives

● **Underline the demonstrative adjective in each sentence. Circle the noun it describes. Then write *near* or *far* to tell its location.**

1. My feet are too big for these shoes.   _____

2. Petra planted those trees last year.   _____

3. This popcorn tastes too salty.   _____

4 The maps in that book have many details.   _____

5. Did you make these muffins?   _____

6. I can't use this pillow because I'm allergic to it.   _____

7. That picture was painted by my mother.   _____

8. Do you see those geese fly overhead?   _____

● **Write a demonstrative adjective to complete each sentence. Use the information in parentheses for the location.**

9. _____ apples are the best for pies. (near)

10. _____ sock has a big hole in it. (far)

11. Nancy painted _____ pictures with watercolors. (far)

12. _____ hot dog needs mustard. (near)

13. Who brought _____ CDs to the party? (far)

14. _____ sandwiches are peanut butter and jelly. (near)

CHAPTER 3

Adjectives That Tell How Many

● **Circle the adjective that tells how many or about how many in each sentence. (Hint: There may be more than one.)**

1. Darryl threw a few pieces of bread to the birds.

2. Six horses galloped across the grassy field.

3. Jayna played first base in both softball games.

4. Several students agreed to share their second drafts with the class.

5. Jackson brought all the trash outside.

6. Kylie invited ten friends to her birthday party.

7. Either dress will be fine for any of the parties.

8. Every night four cats climb the fence and meow.

9. This is my first time rock climbing!

10. Most cars have some special features.

● **Add an adjective that tells how many or about how many. The adjective should go with the noun.**

11. _____ butter   14. _____ tennis balls

12. _____ clothes   15. _____ homework

13. _____ shoe   16. _____ notebooks

CHAPTER 3

Roots

● **Circle the word that correctly completes each sentence. Use your knowledge of roots to choose the correct word.**

1. The nurse uses a (chronometer   thermometer) to check the boy's temperature.

2. An (autograph   autobiography) is a book someone writes about his or her own life.

3. I used (dividers   division) to separate the sections of my report.

4. The tram will (transport   porter) us to the entrance of the amusement park.

5. Her attorney questioned the (credit   credibility) of the witness.

6. Sarah is a (finale   finalist) in the music competition.

● **The Latin root *aqu* means "water." Read the words below and answer the questions. Use a dictionary if you need help.**

| aqueduct | aquatic | aquarium |

7. Which word means—

growing or living in water?   _____

a structure that carries water?   _____

a tank of water that contains plants and animals?   _____

8. Use each word in a sentence that shows you know what the word means.

_____

_____

_____

● **Choose a word that includes the Greek root *geo*, which means "earth." Copy a blank word-analysis chart onto a separate sheet of paper. Complete the chart for your word. For an example of a word-analysis chart, see page 140.**

CHAPTER 3

Subject Complements

● **Identify the position of each italicized adjective. Write *before* or *subject complement* on the line. Then circle the noun the adjective describes.**

1. The *scary* stories held our attention. _____

2. Ally's horse looks *tired*. _____

3. The ocean waves felt *cool* on my legs. _____

4. This is the most *interesting* speech I've heard. _____

5. The clown's dog looked *funny* in a coat and a hat. _____

6. Last night's football game was really *exciting*! _____

7. Did you bake that *delicious* cake? _____

8. After doing well on the test, the students became *confident*. _____

● **Find and circle the nouns you identified above in the word search below. The words can go across, down, or diagonally.**

W	S	I	U	G	T	I	M	A	D	O	G
T	G	A	B	A	W	L	S	I	O	N	E
S	A	W	A	M	S	E	Y	E	S	U	R
S	T	U	D	E	N	T	S	U	A	S	X
A	L	M	O	H	S	H	O	R	S	E	W
S	E	M	N	I	A	I	R	R	K	O	A
R	R	C	R	I	X	L	A	A	I	Y	V
O	I	K	P	S	E	P	C	R	V	E	E
K	S	P	E	E	C	H	S	S	A	M	S
U	S	C	A	T	C	N	E	S	B	E	L

CHAPTER 3

Adjectives That Compare

● **Write the correct comparative or superlative form of the adjective to complete each sentence. Then draw a sketch to show what each sentence means.**

1. small
   This kitten is the _____
   of the litter.
	4. good
	   Her hair looks _____
	   curly than it does straight.

2. happy
   Eric is _____ than his
   friend Lisa.
	5. bad
	   This is the _____ storm
	   I've ever seen!

3. large
   Li grew the _____
   sunflower in the class.
	6. fuzzy
	   My coat is _____
	   than yours.

CHAPTER 3

Combining Sentences and Sentence Parts

● **Combine each pair of sentences into one sentence, using compound sentence parts.**

1. We are making cookies for the bake sale. We are making cupcakes for the bake sale.

   _____

2. Patricia MacLachlan is a popular author. Louis Sachar is a popular author.

   _____

3. At the beach we play volleyball. We swim in the water.

   _____

4. Pedro ate hamburgers at the picnic. Pedro ate potato salad at the picnic.

   _____

5. Raccoons are nocturnal animals. Hamsters are nocturnal animals.

   _____

● **Circle the conjunction that correctly completes each sentence.**

6. The rain poured down on us, (but   or) my new coat kept me dry.

7. We are too late, (but   or) we have arrived very early.

8. We will bring a chocolate cake (or   but) a cherry pie to the potluck dinner.

9. My brother enjoys playing soccer (and   but) basketball on the weekend.

10. Lily wants spaghetti for dinner, (but   and) her mom is making chicken enchiladas.

CHAPTER 3

More, Most and Less, Least

● **Circle the correct form of the adjective to complete each sentence.**

1. I find astronomy (more fascinating   most fascinating) than biology.

2. Hector included the (less important   least important) information of all his research at the end of his newspaper article.

3. My ballet teacher is the (more graceful   most graceful) person I know.

4. Our last math test was the (more difficult   most difficult) one this year.

5. This novel is (less interesting   least interesting) than the author's last book.

6. The (more amazing   most amazing) animal at the zoo was the elephant.

7. Diana chose the (less expensive   least expensive) dress on the rack.

8. Liu's painting is (more vibrant   most vibrant) than Ana's.

9. Our new house is (less spacious   least spacious) than our last one.

10. Brandon is the (more intelligent   most intelligent) student in my class.

● **Write a sentence using the word *less* or *least* with an adjective.**

_____

_____

● **Write a sentence using the word *more* or *most* with an adjective.**

_____

_____

CHAPTER 3

Fewer, Fewest and Less, Least

● Write *fewer, fewest, less,* or *least* to complete each sentence. Then circle the word that each adjective describes.

1. Samantha played _____ games on the computer than her best friend.

2. We received the _____ amount of rain in March.

3. The _____ ranches were located in the northern part of the state.

4. There is _____ butter in the cake than in the cookies.

5. _____ area seems to be available for wildlife in this part of the state than in others.

6. There are _____ grapevines to plant this year than last year.

7. Alicia has _____ eggs in her basket than I do.

8. We spent the _____ time of all on social studies in our study group.

9. My muffin has the _____ raisins!

10. You have _____ understanding of computers than Chad.

11. We saw _____ cats than rabbits in the new shelter.

12. She likes the _____ kinds of food of anyone in her family.

● Now write the first letter of each circled word, in order, on the numbered lines below. If your answers are correct, you will reveal the answer to the riddle.

What has four wheels and flies?

Answer: A _____ _____ _____ _____ _____ _____ _____
             1   2   3   4   5   6   7

_____ _____ _____ _____ _____
    8   9   10   11   12

CHAPTER 3

Filling Out Forms

● Below is a form for Best Buddy Animal Shelter. You are applying to do volunteer work there over the summer. Fill out the form.

Name _____
          FIRST   LAST   MIDDLE INITIAL

Address _____
          NUMBER   STREET

_____
      CITY   STATE   ZIP CODE

Telephone Number   (   ) _____

E-mail Address _____

Do you have any pets? (circle one)   Yes   No

Tell us more about your pets.

_____   _____
Type of animal   Name

_____   _____
Type of animal   Name

What hours will you be available to volunteer each week? (Circle as many as apply.)

Mon.	Tues.	Wed.	Thurs.	Fri.	Sat.
4–6	4–6	4–6	4–6	4–6	9–12
6–8	6–8	6–8	6–8	6–8	12–3

In which jobs are you most interested? (Circle as many as apply.)

Dog walking   Grooming   Feeding

Weekend playtime   Cleaning cages

CHAPTER 3

Interrogative Adjectives

● **Circle the interrogative adjective in each sentence. Underline the noun it goes with.**

1. Whose dogs are running loose in the backyard?

2. What movies are your favorites?

3. Which shoes should you wear in the winter?

4. Whose car is in your driveway?

5. Which instrument do you play in the band?

● **Circle the interrogative adjective that correctly completes each sentence.**

6. (Whose   Which) backpack is on the table—Maria's or Jim's?

7. (Whose   Which) aquarium holds more water—the blue one or the black one?

8. (What   Which) answer did you get to the math problem?

9. (Which   Whose) favorite animal is a hippopotamus?

10. (Which   What) excuse do you have for being late?

● **Write a sentence using each of the following words as interrogative adjectives.**

11. what

_____

12. whose

_____

13. which

_____

Suffixes

● **Combine the word in parentheses with a suffix from the box to make a new word. Write the new word on the line to complete the sentence.**

-ly	-ally	-ize	-y	-ate	-er
-fy	-ish	-ful	-or	-able	

1. Sarah was _____ that she would win first place. (hope)

2. Everyone in my family is _____ talented. (music)

3. Did you know that Michelangelo was a _____ and a _____? (sculpt; paint)

4. That big red chair is more _____ than this wooden one. (comfort)

5. Uncle Sherwin tells lots of _____ jokes over dinner. (fun)

6. My friend Jake acts protectively and _____ toward me. (brother)

7. The baby giggles a lot because she is very _____. (tickle)

8. Please _____ the alarm when you leave the building. (active)

9. Eating a healthy snack will _____ you. (energy)

10. Grandma's big Persian cat is white and _____. (fluff)

11. Thank you for your kind and _____ gift. (thought)

12. The children hope to _____ the park by planting flowers. (beauty)

Past Perfect Tense

● **Underline the verb in the past perfect tense in each sentence.**
  Hint: You will underline two words.

1. I had taken a Spanish class before I traveled to Madrid.

2. By the time we reached the end of the trail, we had hiked nearly six miles.

3. Jonah had finished his chores before he went to the miniature golf park.

4. The cheerleaders had learned two new routines by the second game of the season.

5. Someone had found the keys before we even knew they were missing.

6. Before we moved to California, I had never seen the ocean.

● **Write the verb in parentheses in the past perfect tense to complete**
  each sentence. Hint: You will write two words.

7. I raised my hand once I _____ the solution to
   the problem. (identify)

8. After Tracy _____ the barbecued ribs, she asked
   for a second helping. (taste)

9. Before Manuel gave his speech, he _____ many
   times. (practice)

10. After they _____ a mess in the playroom, the
    children cleaned it up. (make)

11. By the end of the debate Ramona _____ me to
    vote for her. (convince)

12. Before Ricky got a bicycle for his birthday, he _____
    to school every day. (walk)

CHAPTER 4

Future Perfect Tense

● **Write the verb in parentheses in the future perfect tense.**
   Hint: You will write three words.

1. They _____ their reports before the end of class.
   (finish)

2. The birthday party _____ by five o'clock. (end)

3. By noon they _____ baseball for three hours
   straight. (play)

4. By the end of the day Dad _____ the garage. (paint)

5. Hopefully we _____ home before the snowstorm
   hits. (arrive)

6. By next week the students _____ all of their
   speeches. (present)

7. They _____ their rooms before their parents
   get home from work. (clean)

8. These cookies _____ by the time the next batch
   is done. (cool)

9. The performance _____ by 8:00 p.m. (begin)

10. We _____ all of our lines for the play by opening
    night. (learn)

● **Write a sentence with each verb in the future perfect tense.**
   Hint: the verb will have three words.

11. try

_____

12. complete

_____

CHAPTER

4 Dictionary

● **Write each group of entry words in alphabetical order.**

1. silent, sick, simple   _____   _____   _____

2. crackle, crispy, creak   _____   _____   _____

3. brilliant, breakfast, book   _____   _____   _____

4. shower, sheep, steep   _____   _____   _____

5. under, umbrella, useful   _____   _____   _____

● **Circle the word in each row that would appear on a dictionary page with the given guide words.**

6. night/nothing	neat	nice	noise
7. bought/brick	break	beard	bus
8. cake/careful	cured	camel	cable
9. plank/prince	plain	purple	please
10. tank/theater	train	teamwork	trickle

● **Read the dictionary entry. Then write the letter of the dictionary part that matches each description.**

    A   **B** **C**   **D**   **E**
re•cite (ri- ˈsīt) *v.* **1.** to repeat from memory or read aloud publicly *We recite poems*

                                                        F
for the class. **2.** to relate in full **3.** to repeat or answer questions *-ted, -ting*

11. _____ spelling of last syllable with endings added

12. _____ part of speech

13. _____ definition

14. _____ division into syllables

15. _____ dictionary respelling for pronunciation

16. _____ sample phrase or sentence

CHAPTER
4

Linking Verbs

● Underline the linking verb in each sentence. Then determine whether the subject complement is a noun, a pronoun, or an adjective, and circle the corresponding letter.

1. Joshua remained calm this morning.
   n. pronoun
   a. adjective
   t. noun

2. These papers are examples of good writing.
   r. pronoun
   e. adjective
   l. noun

3. Meat is an important source of protein.
   o. pronoun
   s. adjective
   p. noun

4. The winner of the contest was he.
   h. pronoun
   g. adjective
   w. noun

5. Your perfume smells wonderful.
   i. pronoun
   a. adjective
   c. noun

6. Leah has been a wonderful friend.
   d. pronoun
   e. adjective
   b. noun

7. Our new tennis coach will be she.
   e. pronoun
   y. adjective
   r. noun

8. The crisp fall breeze feels chilly.
   s. pronoun
   t. adjective
   n. noun

● Now write the circled letters, in order, on the numbered lines below. If your answers are correct, you will reveal the answer to the riddle.

What one word has the most letters in it?

Answer: _____ _____ _____ _____ _____ _____ _____ _____
         1   2   3   4   5   6   7   8

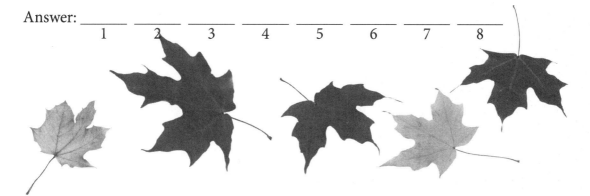

CHAPTER 4

Self-Assessment

● Check *Always*, *Sometimes*, or *Never* to respond to each statement.

Writing	Always	Sometimes	Never
I can identify the features of a description.			
I can use spatial or chronological order to organize the details of a description.			
I can use word webs and Venn diagrams to organize the details for a description.			
I can identify suffixes and use them to create new words.			
I can identify and use the parts of a dictionary entry.			

Grammar	Always	Sometimes	Never
I can identify and use action verbs and being verbs.			
I can identify and use verb phrases and helping verbs.			
I can identify and form the present, present participle, past, and past participle forms of verbs.			
I can identify and form irregular verbs.			
I can identify and form simple tenses of verbs.			
I can identify and form progressive tenses of verbs.			
I can identify and form verbs in the present perfect tense.			
I can identify and form verbs in the past perfect tense.			
I can identify and form verbs in the future perfect tense.			
I can identify and use linking verbs.			

● **Write the most helpful thing you learned in this chapter.**

_____

_____

© Loyola Press

Coordinating Conjunctions

● **Circle the conjunction in each sentence. Underline the two sentence parts it connects. Write *subjects*, *predicates*, or *direct objects* to identify the compound part.**

1. Alaska and Hawaii are states.   _____

2. Mia and Luke rode horses in the parade.   _____

3. Mom bakes cookies and cooks puddings.   _____

4. Brandon or Mike will help us move.   _____

5. My puppy chews bones and old shoes.   _____

6. After school we saw a movie and had dinner.   _____

7. We ate pizza and salad for our meal.   _____

8. My teacher or the coach can start the race.   _____

● **Write a conjunction to connect each sentence pair. Use *or, and,* or *but*.**

9. You should get some rest, _____ you will get sick.

10. Jon's painting was the best, _____ Kevin won the prize for first place.

11. We wrote a letter to our senator, _____ then we all signed it.

12. I wanted to visit France, _____ I went to Spain instead.

CHAPTER 5

Subordinate Conjunctions

● **Circle the subordinate conjunction in each sentence. Then underline the dependent clause once and the independent clause twice.**

1. Brett went home because he was not feeling well.

2. Once the rain stopped, a rainbow lit up the sky.

3. Although he got a leg cramp, Chris finished the game.

4. We cannot start the baseball game until the rain stops.

5. They must finish their tests before the bell rings.

6. Whenever I think of my baby sister, I smile.

7. Let's leave early so we can avoid the traffic.

8. If the car is fixed, we can leave tomorrow.

9. I feel small when I look at a huge, star-filled sky.

10. Since Jeremy moved away, I have felt lonely.

11. Kayla cannot baby-sit because she has plans this weekend.

12. Maria laughs whenever she hears this joke.

Fact and Opinion

● **Write *fact* or *opinion* to identify each statement.**

1. My family went on a trip to Mexico. _____ _____

2. We had a great time on our trip. _____ _____

3. My mother's middle name is Marie. _____

4. I was born on May 15, 1993. _____

5. Mr. Jett is a talented coach and mentor. _____

6. Abraham Lincoln is my favorite president. _____

7. Ten inches of rain fell in Oregon last month. _____

8. My baby sister looks a lot like me. _____

9. Memorial Day is celebrated in May. _____

10. Our new car is candy apple red. _____

● **Choose a subject you are studying in class. On a separate sheet of paper create a Fact-and-Opinion Chart like the one on page 138. Write five facts and five opinions about the subject.**

CHAPTER

5

Interjections

• **Underline the interjection in each sentence. Then write *joy, sorrow, caution, pain, wonder, disgust, surprise,* or *greeting* to identify an emotion expressed by each.**

1. Ugh! This sandwich tastes awful.   _____

2. Fantastic! You are done with your chores.   _____

3. Oh! Those stars are amazing.   _____

4. Good-bye! It was great to see you.   _____

5. Watch out! The sidewalk is slippery.   _____

6. Ouch! That frying pan is hot.   _____

7. Wow! I did not expect to see you today.   _____

8. Cheers! Your concert was wonderful.   _____

• **Write a sentence for each interjection.**

9. Yes! _____

10. Yuck! _____

11. Incredible! _____

12. Careful! _____

Name _____ **Date** _____

Self-Assessment

● Check *Always, Sometimes,* or *Never* to respond to each statement.

Writing	Always	Sometimes	Never
I can identify the features of a book report.			
I can identify and write the important parts of a book report.			
I can identify and revise rambling and run-on sentences.			
I can identify and use words with prefixes.			
I can identify and write facts and opinions.			

Grammar	Always	Sometimes	Never
I can identify and use adverbs of time, place, and manner.			
I can identify and use adverbs that compare.			
I can use troublesome words and negative words.			
I can use *there is/there are* correctly in sentences.			
I can identify and use adverb clauses.			
I can identify and use prepositions and their objects.			
I can identify and use prepositional phrases as adjectives.			
I can identify and use prepositional phrases as adverbs.			
I can identify and use coordinating conjunctions.			
I can identify and use subordinate conjunctions.			
I can identify and use interjections.			

● **Explain how using what you have learned in this chapter can make you a better writer.**

_____

_____

_____

CHAPTER

6 Kinds of Sentences

● Write *declarative, interrogative, imperative,* or *exclamatory* to identify each sentence. Rewrite each sentence to show correct end punctuation.

1. Several hikers climbed up the mountain _____

_____

2. Where is my homework _____

_____

3. That is the most beautiful sunset ever _____

_____

4. Please fasten your seatbelt now _____

_____

5. How do you spell your last name _____

_____

6. The water is too cold for swimming _____

_____

7. Ouch! That sliver really hurts _____

_____

8. Hand me that box of crayons, please _____

_____

● **Choose an activity or sport you really enjoy. On a separate sheet of paper write four sentences about it. Write a declarative, an interrogative, an imperative, and an exclamatory sentence.**

CHAPTER 6 Simple Subjects and Simple Predicates

● **Circle the simple subject in each sentence. Underline the simple predicate.**

1. A gray mist drifted over the frozen pond.

2. The exploratory vehicle moved across the barren landscape of Mars.

3. The scientist slowly poured the chemicals into the test tube.

4. That group of squirrels has gathered all the nuts.

5. Several children might try for a part in the play.

6. The end of the story was a disappointment.

7. The dog's bark scared the young child.

8. Mr. Thomas painted the baby's room blue and yellow.

● **Write a simple subject or a simple predicate on each line to complete the paragraph.**

The puppies _____ quickly. Yesterday _____

could hold one in his hand. Now their furry _____ tumble and

roll across the carpet. My favorite one _____ my face with his

rough tongue. My _____ named the largest puppy Shasta.

Shasta _____ as fast as she can across the room.

Name _____ Date _____

What Makes a Good Tall Tale?

● **Circle the letter of the answer that best completes each statement.**

1. Tall tales feature _____.
   a. a supernatural setting   b. a larger-than-life hero   c. rhymes

2. A tall tale often uses exaggeration and _____ when explaining the plot.
   a. persuasion   b. statistics   c. humor

3. Tall tales often start by telling about the hero's _____.
   a. friends   b. future   c. childhood

4. Tall tales create surprise by using _____.
   a. exaggeration   b. common people   c. familiar objects

5. Often a tall tale will explain how some _____ began.
   a. natural disaster   b. familiar thing   c. superstition

6. The character in a tall tale speaks in a manner that matches the tale's
   _____.
   a. time and place   b. past and future   c. facts and opinions

● **Look at the sample story map on page 137. Copy a blank story map on a separate sheet of paper. Describe characters, settings, and events that you could write about in a tall tale.**

CHAPTER 6

Complete Subjects and Complete Predicates

● Draw one line under the complete subject in each sentence. Draw two lines under the complete predicate.

1. Several large shrubs hid the house from view.

2. Multicolored hot-air balloons drifted into the sky.

3. Our science fiction club will meet on Tuesdays.

4. The ancient Romans used salt as money.

5. The coldest day of the year was in January.

6. A cup of hot cocoa sat on the table.

● Add a complete subject or a complete predicate to finish each sentence. Write *subject* or *predicate* to identify which part you added.

7. Tiny glowing fireflies _____ . _____

8. _____ listened intently to the forest noises. _____

9. _____ made chirping sounds with their wings. _____

10. Our entire group of campers _____ . _____

CHAPTER 6

Direct Objects and Indirect Objects

● Circle the number under the heading that describes the italicized word in each sentence.

	Direct Object	Indirect Object
1. The storm clouds brought the *land* heavy rains.	399	412
2. Our teacher assigned the class a *report* on insects.	98	107
3. My brother sent Aunt Sophie a birthday *card*.	103	212
4. Mr. Jensen gave the *usher* the tickets.	299	326
5 Mother promised *Elena* a new coat for her birthday.	67	275
6. The funny magician taught the children a card *trick*.	697	882
7. Caroline told her best *friend* the secret.	29	199
8. Vicky offered the boy a *dollar* for his drawing.	404	345
9. Mrs. Camillo handed the new *student* a pencil.	210	500
10. The young woman read the group a *story*.	198	701

● **Add together the numbers you circled above. If your answers are correct, the sum will answer the question below.**

How tall is Angel Falls, the tallest waterfall in the world? _____ feet

CHAPTER
6

Writing a
Tall Tale

● **Read each statement about tall tales. Write *true* or *false* for each
statement. If the statement is false, rewrite it to be true.**

1. Tall tale writers choose any subject, even those they know
   nothing about.   _____

   _____

2. Often the first step in writing a tall tale is to choose a hero.   _____

   _____

3. In a tall tale the bigger the exaggeration, the more sad
   the story.   _____

   _____

4. The hero of a tall tale should have a job the writer knows
   something about.   _____

   _____

5. The problem the hero faces should be something that has
   happened in the past.   _____

   _____

6. While the rest of a tall tale is humorous, the solution
   should be serious.   _____

   _____

7. Superlative adjectives, such as *biggest, tallest,* and *longest,*
   have no place in tall tales.   _____

   _____

CHAPTER 6

Subject Complements

● **Circle the subject complement in each sentence. Then write *noun* or *adjective* to identify the word.**

1. Steve was the only player on the soccer field. _____

2. My neighbors are volunteers for the school fundraiser. _____

3. This historic bridge is very scenic. _____

4. The portrait of your grandmother was beautiful. _____

5. Your ankle appears swollen. _____

6. My favorite sport is volleyball. _____

● **Write a sentence that uses each of the following words as a subject complement.**

7. mammal

_____

8. nocturnal

_____

9. hero

_____

10. spectacular

_____

11. subject

_____

12. boring

_____

CHAPTER
6

Sentence Order

● **Write *natural* or *inverted* to identify the word order of each sentence.**

1. Across the prairie galloped a herd of wild horses. _____

2. A large raccoon scurried over the fence. _____

3. Justin's sister took the last piece of cornbread. _____

4. In what year were you born? _____

5. Across the horizon drifted ominous storm clouds. _____

6. The tired hikers rested by the edge of the stream. _____

7. Down tumbled the tower of blocks. _____

8. One jellybean remained at the bottom of the jar. _____

● **Think about a subject you have recently studied in social studies. Write two natural sentences and two inverted sentences about the subject on the lines below.**

9. _____

_____

10. _____

_____

11. _____

_____

12. _____

_____

CHAPTER

6

Figurative Language

● Write *exaggeration, simile,* or *metaphor* to identify the figurative language used in each statement.

1. On the hottest day of the year, tires melted into pools of rubber on the road.

   _____

2. Her eyes fluttered like the wings of an overactive butterfly.

   _____

3. The sunflower grew to the height of a skyscraper.

   _____

4. The steak was so tough, it could have doubled for shoe leather.

   _____

5. The garage is a maze of tools and car parts.

   _____

6. His voice is so loud and booming it sounds like a car alarm.

   _____

7. Sonia's smile is a beacon of light on a dark night.

   _____

8. The skin on his hands was as rough as a piece of sandpaper.

   _____

9. I'm so thirsty I could drink up one of the Great Lakes.

   _____

10. The closet under the stairs is a black hole.

    _____

Name _____   Date _____

CHAPTER 6

Compound Subjects and Compound Predicates

● **Underline the compound subject in each sentence.**

1. Quarters or dollars will go into that vending machine.

2. Hydrogen and oxygen make up a water molecule.

3. Does jelly or butter go better with bread?

4. Sarah or her sister will help you with your homework.

5. Mysteries and science fiction have fascinating plots.

6. Hockey and tennis are my two favorite sports.

● **Combine each pair of sentences into one sentence with a compound predicate. Make sure that the subject and verbs agree.**

7. Brad swam the river. Brad hiked the canyon.

   _____

8. Sedimentary rock is formed over time. Sedimentary rock contains many types of fossils.

   _____

9. Roses smell wonderful. Roses brighten up a room.

   _____

10. The beach is very sandy. The beach receives much sunlight.

    _____

CHAPTER 6

Compound Direct Objects

● **Underline the compound direct object in each sentence.**

1. My family will visit Canada or Alaska this summer.

2. Lucy bought bananas and watermelon at the grocery store.

3. This author writes poetry and fiction.

4. Do you prefer New York or New Orleans?

5. I greeted friends and relatives after my performance.

6. Our teacher provided watercolors and brushes for the project.

● **Write a compound object to complete each sentence.**

7. My older sister bought _____ at the store.

8. The new puppy chewed _____ .

9. For dinner, I think I will prepare _____ .

10. We sold _____ at our garage sale.

11. Mr. Sanchez may purchase _____ .

12. I cleaned my _____ .

CHAPTER
6

Homophones

● **Circle the homophone that correctly completes each sentence.**

1. Our (principal   principle) announced the guest speaker at the school assembly.

2. (Break   Brake) carefully when you are riding the bicycle downhill.

3. Have you seen (there   their) new home?

4. Mom, can you (sew   sow) my costume for the play?

5. We admired the new sailboat docked at the (peer   pier).

6. Take a (peek   peak) at the gift we bought for our aunt.

● **Use the homophones you did not use above. Write a sentence that uses each correctly.**

7. _____

8. _____

9. _____

10. _____

11. _____

12. _____

CHAPTER 6 Compound Subject Complements

● **Underline the compound subject complement in each sentence. Write *nouns* or *adjectives* to identify each subject complement.**

1. She appeared anxious and excited before her solo.

   _____

2. The English actress is well-known and respected.

   _____

3. The only vegetables in the salad were lettuce and radishes.

   _____

4. My favorite fruits are strawberries and watermelon.

   _____

5. Tom's brother is a swimmer and runner.

   _____

6. Our breakfast was toast and bananas.

   _____

7. The buzzing sound was constant and annoying.

   _____

8. Mother's cherry pie can be tart or sweet.

   _____

9. Juan's favorite movies are comedies and mysteries.

   _____

10. The automobile in the ad was sleek and shiny.

    _____

11. The path through the park is long and winding.

    _____

12. The food at that new restaurant could be good or bad.

    _____

Compound Sentences

CHAPTER 6

● **Draw one line under the complete subjects in the independent clauses in each compound sentence. Draw two lines under the complete predicates. Circle the conjunction or semicolon.**

1. I enjoy many kinds of books, but my brother only likes science fiction.

2. The painting was original and creative; it won first prize.

3. He dusted the shelf, and the books fell over.

4. Grandfather may take a plane, or my father may drive him here.

5. Maurice will not leave until noon, but he should arrive before the start of the game.

● **Write an independent clause and include a conjunction or semicolon to create a compound sentence.**

6. Safety goggles will protect your eyes _____ .

7. Our break is in early spring _____ .

8. There was a full moon last week _____ .

9. Peter ran out of paper _____ .

10. Brian wanted to join us _____ .

11. Everyone attended the concert _____ .

CHAPTER

6 Nonsense Verse

● **Match a word or phrase from the word box to each statement. You will use each word or phrase once.**

humor	rhyme scheme	couplet
meter	syllables	made-up words

1. _____ Nonsense verse often uses this to entertain the reader.

2. _____ In this type of poetry each pair of lines rhymes.

3. _____ This is a pattern of stressed syllables in a poem.

4 _____ This is the pattern of lines that rhyme in a poem.

5. _____ In a word with more than one of these, one is stressed more than the others.

6. _____ A poet may create these as part of a nonsense poem. You would never find them in a dictionary.

● **Choose an animal, a place, and a person. Write a rhyming couplet that features these three things.**

_____

_____

_____

_____

_____

CHAPTER

6

Complex Sentences

● **Underline the adverb clause in each sentence.**

1. After she finished her homework, Janna practiced the piano.

2. When we heard the good news, we jumped for joy.

3. We plan to visit Yellowstone National Park before we travel to California.

4. Since summer ended, Manuel has been waiting for the soccer season.

5. We cannot begin the show until Dana and David arrive.

6. While it was snowing, the children were catching snowflakes on their tongues.

7. Toby has wanted to play baseball since he was a child.

8. We all congratulated the winner after the race was finished.

● **Add an adverb clause that tells when to each sentence.**

9. He received the prize _____ .

10. Jamie talked on the telephone _____ .

11. _____ , my family helped me.

Name _____ **Date** _____

Self-Assessment

● Check *Always, Sometimes,* or *Never* to respond to each statement.

Writing	Always	Sometimes	Never
I can identify a tall tale and its features.			
I can identify and use character, problem/solution, and everyday language in a tall tale.			
I can identify and use figurative language.			
I can identify homophones and use them correctly.			
I can identify and write nonsense verse.			

Grammar	Always	Sometimes	Never
I can identify, use, and punctuate the four kinds of sentences.			
I can identify and use simple subjects and predicates.			
I can identify and use complete subjects and predicates.			
I can identify and use direct and indirect objects.			
I can identify and use subject complements.			
I can identify and use natural and inverted word order in sentences.			
I can identify and use compound subjects and compound predicates.			
I can identify and use compound direct objects.			
I can identify and use compound subject complements.			
I can identify and use compound sentences with conjunctions and semicolons.			
I can identify and use complex sentences.			

● **Explain how using a variety of sentence lengths and types can make your writing more interesting.**

_____

_____

CHAPTER 7

End Punctuation

● **Add end punctuation to each sentence. Then write** *declarative,* *imperative, interrogative,* **or** *exclamatory* **to identify the sentence.**

1. Carry the boxes up the stairs   _____

2. Did you meet the new math teacher   _____

3. Wow! This news is so surprising   _____

4. Did you watch the baseball game   _____

5. Please move those desks over by the door   _____

6. How many marbles are in the bag   _____

7. Maya's kitten is hiding behind the chair   _____

8. My baby sister was born in May of last year _____

9. Hey, watch out for those icy steps   _____

10. Several people watched the soccer game last night _____

● **On a separate sheet of paper write one declarative, one interrogative, one imperative, and one exclamatory sentence about an activity you enjoy. Use correct end punctuation for each sentence.**

CHAPTER 7

Commas in Series

● Add commas to separate words in a series. Then write *nouns, verbs,* or *adjectives* to identify the words.

1. Justin can be intelligent funny and interesting.   _____

2. We will shop pack and clean before our trip.   _____

3. Amy Jake and Leah are joining the club.   _____

4. The planets Earth Mercury and Venus are closest
   to the sun.   _____

5. The tiny kitten sat purred and curled into a ball.   _____

6. The slick cold and icy streets were dangerous
   for driving.   _____

7. Tim's brother studies math biology and art.   _____

8. I can see rocks trees and several animals
   in the valley.   _____

9. The audience laughed chortled and giggled
   during the play.   _____

10. The ocean breeze feels salty clean and cool
    on my skin.   _____

11. The snow felt wet cold and heavy.   _____

12. I prefer to read mysteries comics and collections
    of poetry.   _____

CHAPTER 7

What Makes Good Persuasive Writing?

● **Circle the letter of the answer that correctly completes each statement.**

1. For a persuasive essay the topic should have two _____.
   a. paragraphs   b. opposing views   c. conclusions

2. Your viewpoint on a topic is called your _____.
   a. position   b. introduction   c. example

3. In the introduction of a persuasive essay you should grab the reader's attention and _____.
   a. make him or her laugh   b. state your position   c. summarize your ideas

4. The body of a persuasive essay is where you use details to _____.
   a. convince your audience   b. repeat your position   c. distract the reader

5. The conclusion to a persuasive essay should _____.
   a. share new ideas   b. make the audience angry   c. summarize your ideas

● **Write a reason for and a reason against each position below.**

6. Students should be able to choose their own school hours.

   _____

   _____

7. Cats are better pets than dogs.

   _____

   _____

Commas with Conjunctions

CHAPTER 7

● **Add commas to the following sentences if needed. Not all sentences need commas. Circle the conjunctions.**

1. Many people in our community live in town but some of them live in the country.

2. We want to visit the zoo but we also want to see that new movie.

3. Mina practiced very hard for auditions and we hope she gets the part.

4. You can find the books in my backpack or my locker.

5. Brianna can go to the party or she can stay home and study.

6. The ocean waves crashed and tumbled on the shore.

● **Rewrite the following pairs of sentences as compound sentences. Use conjunctions and commas where needed.**

7. The wind blew hard outside. We felt warm anyway.

_____

_____

8. My family saw lots of puppies in the shelter. We decided to adopt one.

_____

_____

Name _____ Date _____

CHAPTER 7

Direct Address and Yes and No

● **Rewrite the sentences. Add commas where needed.**

1. Yes there are more than six planets in our solar system.

   _____

2. Maria will you help me research how a star is formed?

   _____

3. Tanner I cannot study with you this weekend.

   _____

4. I do believe Sean that class begins tomorrow morning.

   _____

5. I do not know the answer to that question Mrs. Shields.

   _____

6. Yes I saw the shooting stars over the treetops.

   _____

7. Our conversation last night Michael made me very happy.

   _____

8. Yes I can help you work in the garden this weekend Grandma.

   _____

● **Think of a topic you are studying in class. Write an example exchange between a teacher and a student or two students. Use direct address in a question, and *Yes* or *No* in the answer.**

Question: _____

Answer: _____

CHAPTER 7

Writing a Persuasive Article

● **Read each pair of ideas. Circle the letter of the most persuasive argument in each pair.**

1. A. The new animal shelter would help the many homeless animals roaming the streets.
   B. The new shelter would be a safe haven for 20 percent more animals than there is currently room for in our city and also provide a place for adoption.

2. A. A lower speed limit is needed because accidents increased 45 percent when the limit went from 55 miles per hour to 65 miles per hour.
   B. We should have a lower speed limit because driving fast is unsafe.

3. A. Kids are smarter today than they used to be, so the voting age should be decreased from 18 to 16.
   B. As a result of television and computers teenagers know a lot about world events. Therefore, the voting age should be changed from 18 to 16.

4. A. School should start later in the day because most teenagers like to stay up late.
   B. Because medical experts have proved that teenagers requires more sleep to accommodate rapid growth, school should start later in the day.

● **Rewrite each opinion. Add details to make it more persuasive.**

5. Dogs are useful to humans.

   _____

6. Tennis is good for your health.

   _____

● **Persuasive writing is best when supported with facts and statistics. Choose a topic for a persuasive essay. On a separate sheet of paper create a K-W-L Chart like the one on page 138. Write what you know about the topic and what you want to know. Research some facts to support your position. Add them to the last column of the chart.**

CHAPTER 7

Apostrophes

● **Rewrite each group of words using an apostrophe to show possession. The first one is done for you.**

1. the tests of the students
   <u>the students' tests</u>

2. the backpack of Anna
   _____

3. the paws of the puppies
   _____

4. the pool of the family
   _____

5. the houses of my neighbors
   _____

6. the children of the Smiths
   _____

7. the leaves of the tree
   _____

8. the uniforms of the nurse
   _____

● **Rewrite each group of words to form a contraction.**

9. we have
   _____

10. I will
    _____

11. I am
    _____

12. there is
    _____

13. are not
    _____

14. have not
    _____

15. do not
    _____

16. they are
    _____

CHAPTER

7

Capital Letters

● **Rewrite each sentence. Add capital letters where needed.**

1. memorial day is in the month of may each year.

   _____

2. hanukkah and christmas are both celebrated in december.

   _____

3. i will visit washington, d.c., with my parents in the summer.

   _____

4. the horse named falling star won the kentucky derby.

   _____

5. mr. chang is taking us to the los angeles museum of art on monday.

   _____

6. the thompsons moved from oak street to rosebud avenue.

   _____

7. enrique and julia take the bus to st. mary's middle school.

   _____

8. my little brother devon was born on a friday.

   _____

CHAPTER

7

Expanding Sentences

● **Write two vivid adjectives to describe each noun in different ways.**

1. beach _____   _____

2. sky _____   _____

3. snow _____   _____

4. bear _____   _____

● **Write two vivid adverbs to describe each verb.**

5. laugh _____   _____

6. study _____   _____

7. jump _____   _____

8. scream _____   _____

● **Rewrite these sentences, adding vivid adjectives, adverbs, and prepositional phrases to make them more interesting.**

9. The baby cried. _____

_____.

10. Children are playing. _____

_____.

11. Horses galloped. _____

_____.

12. Bread is baking. _____

_____.

CHAPTER 7

Titles

● **Rewrite each title. Add capital letters where needed. Use underlining for italicized titles.**

1. *sports illustrated for kids* (magazine) _____

2. "the secret life of killer whales" (article) _____

3. *a comedy of errors* (play) _____

4. "little boy blue" (poem) _____

5. *san francisco chronicle* (newspaper) _____

6. "jewels in the sky" (short story) _____

7. *the witch of blackbird pond* (novel) _____

8. "if i had a brontosaurus" (poem) _____

● **Write a sentence that includes a title for each example. Be sure to capitalize the titles correctly.**

9. Your favorite movie

_____

10. Your favorite book

_____

11. Your favorite song

_____

CHAPTER 7

Other Uses of Capital Letters

● **Rewrite each sentence. Use capital letters where needed.**

1. the east is a beautiful place to visit in the fall.

    _____

2. o, katrina! your speech was so funny.

    _____

3. "this is the day!" mark exclaimed happily.

    _____

4. tara and i traveled to the south to visit our grandparents.

    _____

5. jason asked, "would you like me to help you wash the dishes?"

    _____

6. "oh, terri, thanks for your help," i added with a smile.

    _____

● **Rewrite each name. Use initials in place of the words in italics.**

7. *Alice Annabel* Moon   _____

8. *Jonathan Thomas* Brenner   _____

9. *Jeffrey Steven* Chandler   _____

10. Ms. *Jolayna Marie* McKinney _____

CHAPTER

7

Antonyms

● **Write two antonyms for each word below.**

1. finish _____ _____

2. dry _____ _____

3. soft _____ _____

4. break _____ _____

5. quiet _____ _____

6. gloomy _____ _____

7. generous _____ _____

8. terrible _____ _____

● **In each line, circle all possible antonyms for the italicized word.**

9. *strong*   weak   sorry   flimsy   powerful   sturdy   fragile

10. *give*   provide   share   take   grab   seize   thank

11. *bottom*   under   summit   behind   top   restore   peak

12. *identical*   same   different   varied   twin   diverse   solid

CHAPTER 7 Abbreviations

● **Draw a line to match each abbreviation with the word or phrase it replaces.**

1. AD	a. December
2. Dec.	b. Junior
3. Dr.	c. Februrary
4. Jr.	d. Thursday
5. p.m.	e. inch
6. Thurs.	f. anno Domini
7. Feb.	g. Doctor
8. mm	h. California
9. in.	i. millimeter
10. Gov.	j. ante meridiem (before noon)
11. BC	k. Boulevard
12. CA	l. Governor
13. Blvd.	m. post meridiem (after noon)
14. a.m.	n. before Christ

CHAPTER 7

Direct Quotations

● **Rewrite each sentence. Add the correct punctuation and capital letters where needed.**

1. look out for that falling branch! I shouted from across the yard.

_____

2. Mr. Taylor added please have your homework done by Friday.

_____

3. do you think you can finish the hike? the camp ranger asked.

_____

4. well Miranda replied i would like to at least give it a try.

_____

5. wow! Terrell exclaimed that building is really tall!

_____

6. Put your muddy boots on the porch Sam's mother instructed.

_____

7. Gina asked is the baby still asleep in her crib?

_____

8. shh! I whispered we don't want to wake her up, do we?

_____

© Loyola Press

CHAPTER
7

Library

● **Write *fiction, nonfiction,* or *reference* to identify in which section of the library you would find the following books.**

1. *Ramona the Pest* by Beverly Cleary _____

2. *Merriam Webster's Collegiate Dictionary* _____

3. *Romeo and Juliet* by William Shakespeare _____

4. *Facts about Arabian Horses* by Jenna Sherrill _____

5. *Great Battles of World War II* by Dale Lerner _____

6. *World Atlas* _____

7. *Where the Red Fern Grows* by Wilson Rawls _____

8. *Farmer's Almanac* _____

● **On a separate sheet of paper write each list in the order in which they would appear in a card catalog.**

9. **By Title**	10. **By Subject**	11. **By Author**
Funny Bones	Planes	Smith, Gary
A Tiny Treehouse	Continents	Lorenzo, Mario
The Lighthouse Mysteries	Wildcats	McKinney, Morgan
Gregory the Great	Ocean Life	Bingham, Cheryl

CHAPTER 7

Addresses and Letters

● Rewrite the parts of the business letter. Add capital letters and punctuation where needed.

1995 mulberry avenue _____

sherrill ny 10011 _____

march 10 2005 _____

_____ mrs kuro tanaka

_____ new city botanical gardens

_____ 8843 lake street

_____ miami fl 55395

_____ dear mrs tanaka

_____ sincerely yours

_____ ms. tammy stone

● On a separate sheet of paper use the information above to write a letter for Tammy Stone requesting a catalog from the botanical gardens.

Self-Assessment

● **Check Always, Sometimes, or Never to respond to each statement.**

Writing	Always	Sometimes	Never
I can identify the features of persuasive writing.			
I can identify and write a position, introduction, body, and conclusion for a persuasive article.			
I can use adjectives, adverbs, and prepositional phrases to expand sentences.			
I can identify and use antonyms.			
I can use library skills.			

Grammar	Always	Sometimes	Never
I can identify and use end punctuation.			
I can identify and use commas in series.			
I can identify and use commas with conjunctions.			
I can identify and use commas in direct address and with *Yes* and *No*.			
I can identify and use apostrophes.			
I can identify and use capital letters in sentences and proper nouns.			
I can identify and use capital letters in titles.			
I can identify and use capital letters to begin direct quotations, for the pronoun *I*, and the interjection *O*.			
I can identify and use abbreviations.			
I can identify and use correct punctuation in direct quotations.			
I can identify and use correct punctuation in letters.			

● **Write the most helpful thing you learned in this chapter.**

_____

_____

CHAPTER 8

Subjects, Predicates, Direct Objects, Modifiers

● **Diagram the sentences.**

1. Hawks soar.

2. Spencer drank juice.

3. A little bird is chirping softly.

4. The enormous car stopped quickly.

CHAPTER 8 Indirect Objects

● **Diagram the sentences.**

1. Al sold his neighbor a bicycle.

2. Dad gave my mother flowers.

3. His sister bought us a new magazine.

4. The boy owes his friend some money.

CHAPTER 8

What Makes a Good Research Report?

● Read each unfinished sentence. Next to each number, write the letter of a phrase from the phrase box that correctly completes each sentence.

Phrase Box

1. _____ The purpose of a research report is to

2. _____ Because a report will reflect your interest and enthusiasm,

3. _____ Use questions as you do research to

4. _____ Information for your report can

5. _____ Develop a topic sentence to help you

6. _____ An effective introduction

7. _____ A good conclusion

a. narrow down the information you will include.

b. help you decide which information is important and which is not.

c. come from a variety of sources such as books, reference materials, and Web sites.

d. give factual, organized information about a topic.

e. choose a topic that interests you.

f. often summarizes the topic of the report.

g. catches the reader's attention.

Name _____ **Date** _____

CHAPTER

8

Subject Complements

● **Diagram the sentences.**

1. A kangaroo is a mammal.

2. Grapes are a healthy snack.

3. The dictionary was heavy.

4. My best friend is a fast runner.

CHAPTER 8

Prepositional Phrases

● **Diagram the sentences.**

1. The kitten jumped over the box.

2. I read a book about bats.

3. The frightened puppy was hiding under the bed.

4. A patch of blue appeared through the clouds.

CHAPTER 8

Gathering and Organizing Information

● **Rewrite the information to make a Works Cited page for a report.
Then number the sources to show the correct alphabetical order.**

1. _____ An article titled "Search for the Northwest Passage" found on
May 6, 2004, at this Web site address: www.historyfacts.org/Explorers.
No author given.

_____

2. _____ A book titled *Voyages of Henry Hudson* by Walter M. Little, published by
New Learning Publications in New York, in 2002.

_____

3. _____ A Web site article "English Explorers" from www.csus.edu/Explorers/
Great Britain, by Charles S. Raleigh. Found on April 12, 2004.

_____

4. _____ A book titled *Expeditions to North America* by Sarah Wilkins,
published by Searchlight Books in Chicago, in 2004.

_____

5. _____ An encyclopedia entry titled "Henry Hudson" in the *New Book of
Knowledge* encyclopedia, 2002 edition.

_____

● **Find two sources of information about the explorer Henry Hudson. Make
a note card for one fact you find in each source. Write the sources of
information on the note cards. Share your note cards with a classmate
and compare the facts and sources you found.**

CHAPTER

8 **Interjections**

● **Diagram the sentences.**

1. Hey, I finished my homework.

2. Oh! This problem is difficult.

3. Yikes, he left his backpack in the classroom.

4. Shh! You will scare the timid deer.

CHAPTER 8

Compound Subjects and Compound Predicates

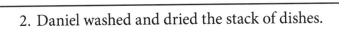

● **Diagram the sentences.**

1. Pam and Jim drove to the city.

2. Daniel washed and dried the stack of dishes.

3. Evan or Roger can bring me the tickets for the concert.

4. The excited baseball fans clapped and cheered.

CHAPTER

8

Outlines

● **Read each statement about outlines. Write *true* or *false* for each. If the statement is false, rewrite it to make it true.**

1. An outline is the final form of a research report. _____

   _____

2. An outline usually shows ideas in their order
   of importance. _____

   _____

3. Main ideas are labeled with lowercase letters. _____

   _____

4. Each main idea may become a topic sentence in your report. _____

   _____

5. Because your outline is not a part of your final report, it
   does not need to be neat. _____

   _____

6. Subtopics are related to the main idea, and there are
   always two or more subtopics under each main idea. _____

   _____

7. Do not mix sentences, phrases, and words in an outline. _____

   _____

● **With a partner choose a topic you would both like to research. Look
at the sample outline on page 139. Copy a blank outline on a separate
sheet of paper. Do research for your topic. Complete the outline by
listing main ideas and related details for a report topic.**

© Loyola Press

Compound Direct Objects and Indirect Objects

● **Diagram the sentences.**

1. The children made signs and invitations.

2. These colorful birds eat fresh fruit and tasty seeds.

3. Mom gave Tony and me a dollar for our lunch.

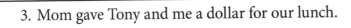

4. The principal awarded the older boy and the younger girl a prize.

CHAPTER 8

Compound Subject Complements

● **Diagram the sentences.**

1. His new puppy is soft and cuddly.

2. The last children in line are Susan and her brother.

3. The new soccer coach is strict but fair.

4. My favorite fruits from Hawaii are ripe guavas and juicy pineapples.

CHAPTER 8

Compound Words

● **Create compound words by writing a word from Column B next to the appropriate word in Column A.**

Column A

1. fire _____

2. arrow _____

3. sun _____

4. every _____

5. skate _____

6. life _____

Column B

head

body

like

place

board

rise

● **Use a compound word from above to complete each sentence.**

7. Our class took a vote, and _____ voted to play soccer.

8. A hiker found a Native American _____ by the creek.

9. The painting was so _____ it looked like a photograph.

10. We placed several logs into the _____.

11. Dad woke us up early so we could watch the _____.

12. Jesse got a new _____ for his birthday.

CHAPTER

Compound Sentences

● **Diagram the sentences.**

1. I remembered my homework, but I left my lunch on the counter.

2. Steve's eyes are blue, and Terri's eyes are deep green.

3. You can open your birthday presents, or we can play some fun games.

4. The dog behind the fence barked fiercely, so we moved away from the rickety fence.

© Loyola Press

Adverb Clauses

● **Diagram the sentences.**

1. Unless the rain stops, we will cancel our baseball game.

2. When the student finishes his test, he will place it into the basket.

3. Traffic was a mess because snow thickly blanketed the city streets.

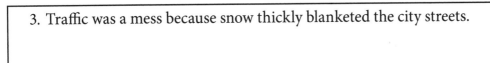

4. The large dog ate three biscuits after he raced around the park.

CHAPTER 8

Library Reference Materials

● **Match a word from the word box to each statement. You will use each word only one time.**

reference	index	keyword	atlas
almanac	periodicals	articles	encyclopedia

1. _____ This is a reference source that contains articles about people, places, things, and events. Topics are organized alphabetically.

2. _____ This section of the library contains books that cannot be checked out. Each source has a special purpose.

3. _____ This contains maps that may show geographical features, political features, historic locations, climates, and populations.

4. _____ Using this will help you locate a specific topic in an encyclopedia.

5. _____ Each of these in an encyclopedia may be illustrated with pictures, diagrams, and maps.

6. _____ This contains very recent facts and statistics. It is published every year.

7. _____ These are published periodically and provide up-to-date information.

8. _____ Some encyclopedia or periodical sets have one of these to help you locate volumes that contain certain keywords.

CHAPTER 8

Diagramming Review

● **Diagram the sentences.**

1. Wow, the heartbeat of a tiny hummingbird is rapid and steady.

2. The campers pitched the tent after they located a flat spot.

3. The cheerleaders will perform a new routine, and the band will play a lively march.

4. The students in the music class sang and played, and the audience gave the performances a loud round of applause.

CHAPTER
8

Self-Assessment

● Check *Always, Sometimes,* or *Never* to respond to each statement.

Writing	Always	Sometimes	Never
I can identify the features of a research report.			
I can gather and organize information for a research report and correctly cite my sources.			
I can identify the parts of an outline and use it to organize information.			
I can identify and use compound words.			
I can identify and use different library reference materials.			

Grammar	Always	Sometimes	Never
I can diagram subjects, predicates, direct objects, and modifiers.			
I can diagram sentences with indirect objects.			
I can diagram sentences with nouns and adjectives used as subject complements.			
I can diagram sentences with prepositional phrases.			
I can diagram sentences with interjections.			
I can diagram sentences with compound subjects and compound predicates.			
I can diagram sentences with compound direct objects and indirect objects.			
I can diagram sentences with compound subject complements.			
I can diagram compound sentences.			
I can diagram sentences with adverb clauses.			

● **Explain how learning to diagram the parts of sentences will help you be a better writer.**

_____

_____

_____

Story Map

Characters: me, my mom, my little brother

Setting: a pumpkin patch at a farm

Main Events:
1. rode into patch on a wagon pulled by a tractor
2. picked our pumpkins
3. tractor driver forgot us
4. walked 1 mile back to farm

Ending: got free pumpkins and a homemade dinner from the farmer's wife

Sequence Chart

Topic: How to Braid

1. Divide hair into three sections.

2. Cross the right section over the middle. Pull tight.

3. Cross the left section over the middle. Pull tight.

4. Keep overlapping right to left until you get to the end of the hair.

5. Fasten with a hair band.

Conclusion: You can make one big braid or many small braids, depending on how many sections of hair you braid.

K-W-L Chart

What I Know

Jackie Robinson was the first African-American baseball player in the major leagues.

What I Want to Know

1. When did he play in his first game?
2. Who signed him?
3. Was he accepted at first?

What I Learned

1. April 15, 1947
2. Branch Rickey, president of the Brooklyn Dodgers
3. No. He got hate mail and some pitchers tried to hit him with the ball, but he was finally accepted.
4. He helped fight for civil rights his whole adult life.

Fact-and-Opinion Chart

Fact

In 1997 scientists discovered fossilized dinosaur eggs in Argentina.

The eggs were from a titanosaur.

The eggs measured 18 inches long.

Opinion

Dinosaurs were cool.

Someday scientists will know everything about dinosaurs.

Studying dinosaurs is exciting.

Outline

Title: __Maps__

I. Road Map
  A. shows roads in an area
  B. used to find locations and distances

II. Political Map
  A. shows political borders
  B. often shows names
      1. cities
      2. states
      3. countries
  C. often shows bodies of water
      1. major rivers
      2. lakes
      3. oceans

III. Physical Map
  A. shows natural borders
  B. shows physical features
      1. mountains
      2. plains
      3. deserts
      4. valleys

Word/Idea Web

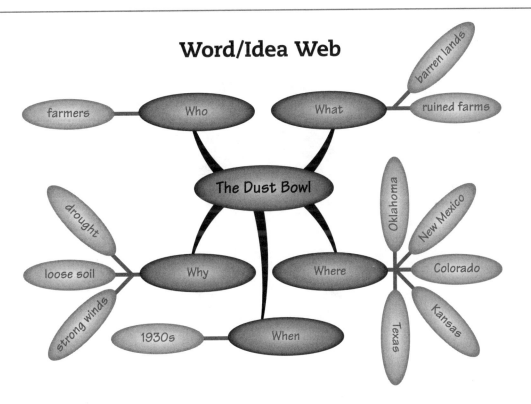

© Loyola Press

Word-Analysis Chart

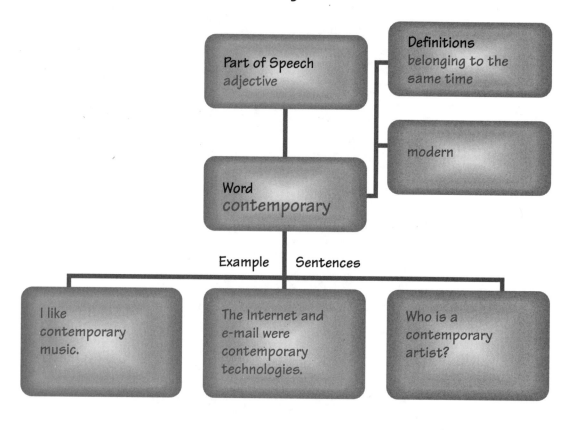

Part of Speech
adjective

Definitions
belonging to the same time

modern

Word
contemporary

Example   Sentences

I like contemporary music.

The Internet and e-mail were contemporary technologies.

Who is a contemporary artist?

Five-Senses Chart

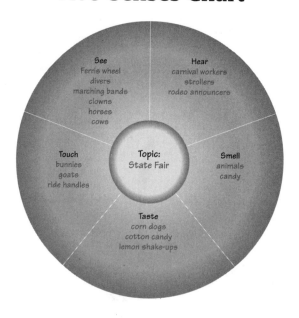

See
Ferris wheel
divers
marching bands
clowns
horses
cows

Hear
carnival workers
strollers
rodeo announcers

Touch
bunnies
goats
ride handles

Topic:
State Fair

Smell
animals
candy

Taste
corn dogs
cotton candy
lemon shake-ups